Conversations with Heaven
Robert Mason

CONTENTS

Introduction

My name is Robert Mason I am a clairvoyant and I can see and hear the Angels, especially our Guardian Angels. I feel them with me every day.

Within this book are messages that were recorded as they were given to me from conversations I have with Angels and Higher Beings from Heaven. I also include "Spiritual insights" given to me that I have expressed as poetic messages. The unconditional love and beauty of Heaven and the Angels impacts me constantly. The conversations are enabled through the technique of "Thought Projection" which is the same way that souls communicate in Heaven.

I am an acclaimed clairvoyant-medium and psychic and have given over 9000 readings. I opened-up a clairvoyant ability that runs in my family through my spiritual research. In the past ten years I have taken my research to a new level in conversations with the Guardian Angels and higher beings in Heaven. The conversations are enabled through thought projection. In the spiritual realm souls communicate using thought projection. It is rapid, and communications that would take some time in language can be made and received instantly as a sudden knowingness.

As a clairvoyant I can see through to Heaven. I sense the Guardian Angels who bring messages and visions from loved ones and friends in Heaven. Messages from Heaven are brought through in normal conversation and can bring wonderful reassurance. I had been a Christian most of my life, and trained as a Methodist Preacher until I realised that I was better helping people with my clairvoyant gift and spiritual understanding. The knowledge I impart has been given to me by Heaven so that people may feel more positive about their life and find true fulfilment. The knowledge is not connected with any religious beliefs and is spiritually good and safe.

CHAPTER ONE

Do we have a Soul?

Question: "Do we have a soul?"

"You are a soul. The "Me" or "I am" is an eternal soul. You are a conscious energy, born out of the dimension of conscious energy – the Spiritual Realm, your true home."

Question to Heaven: "What is our soul?"
Answer from Heaven: "Soul is an energy made of the energy of the spiritual dimension. With human physical senses people are unable to detect energies that are from the spiritual dimension. People are unable to see, feel, touch, hear or smell soul energy but that doesn't mean to say that soul energy doesn't exist. It is very real, and soul is the "I am" inside all human beings. Soul is a conscious energy of the spiritual dimension. All energies move and behave in certain ways. All souls have a unique identity within the ultimate state of consciousness, the "I Am". Without the human body souls are intelligent and possess memory and character attributes. Souls are a part of the ultimate intelligence of all universes without which there would be no creation, no purpose, no ambition, no anything."

Ancient civilisations believed

*in spiritual entities and
subsequently religions evolved*

Throughout history, and dating back to the earliest civilisations, societies have held beliefs in an unseen spiritual dimension and that human beings have a soul. Perception of the truth seems to have been clouded by humans controlling others and spelling out their own version of religion, spiritual ceremonies, and rituals. However, if we are biological computers with no soul, it would be unlikely that human beings would have, so widely across different societies, continents and across different time periods, come up with the concept of an unseen spiritual dimension. There would have been no need for such a concept. Instead, human beings, without doubt, have consistently felt their spirituality and spiritual forces at work in nature. The ability for humans to have these feelings shows our spirituality as a major factor in understanding who we are.

Human activity

Human activity offers overwhelming evidence of the human soul. If we had no soul and were nothing more than organic computers, we would not have any need to explore, seek adventure, and pursue new experiences. We would not seek entertainment or become bored when we have nothing interesting to do. The human soul expresses the person inside throughout life. Our art, music, literature, and poetry are all expressions of the soul.

Emotions

Without a soul we would not feel emotions. Our brain may trigger physical and emotional reactions such as tears when we are sad or a raised voice when we are angry. However, it is our soul, the "I am" inside that triggers the brain.

There has been an upsurge in interest in ghost hunting and the paranormal, with many television programmes and films being produced by professional ghost hunting teams.

The reason for the upsurge in interest is that hauntings often create paranormal phenomena that can be picked up by the human senses and by scientific instruments. Ghost hunters may claim that they are seeking proof of an Afterlife and the continued existence of the human soul beyond physical death by trying to obtain evidence of paranormal activity.

Ghosts and poltergeists tend to create the most noticeable phenomena, yet such phenomena are only produced by a tiny minority of souls. Most souls seem to produce no phenomena after physical death, although some unusual phenomena in the form of "Signs" can be experienced within a week or so of death. We are a soul energy temporarily dwelling in the physical body of a human being. There are reasons that we are denied a conscious memory of existence in a place that might be called "Heaven" before birth. Our soul memory is deliberately blanked off before birth so that memories of our previous existence, such as a past life, do not interfere with our present life.

The Human Brain

My research into the nature of the human brain from a spiritual perspective is important because the knowledge aids our understanding of paranormal phenomena.

Computers: It is only with the advent of the computer age, and the increased sophistication of computer memory, operating systems and software that we may allow ourselves to see the brain as a biological supercomputer.

Within the brain there are different areas that each have their own purpose. These include pre-programmed areas that control the function of the bodily organs, especially noticeable with the heart rate and lungs.

Other areas control our pre-programmed instinctive behaviors. We have parts of the brain that store long-term and short-term memory. These areas are not pre-programmed with ready-made memories. They are blank, almost like a blank computer memory drive, ready to accept new memories as we begin life's adventure.

Spiritual Beliefs

Religions generally preach that we each have a soul that is our true inner spiritual self. They also teach many different versions of a spiritual realm, as another dimension.

Within this book I accept that humanity throughout several thousand years of recorded history has almost consistently held spiritual beliefs. If we are just flesh and blood, then how can humanity hold the concepts and generate feelings of a spiritual dimension?

It can be logically concluded that within our brain is the place where our soul energy meets and joins with the biological computer of our brain.

The human brain has the extraordinary capability to act as a link between two dimensions of the spiritual and physical universes. What other organ, computer or machine on Earth has that capability?

As human beings our soul energy links so perfectly with our brain that we may forget that we are soul and feel at one with our physical identity.

We become one with our brain and yet our brain biological memory banks are newly created and hold no memory data. We therefore cannot retrieve memories of who we are and where we came from as a soul. All that we can experience is to feel within our soul that there perhaps is a bigger spiritual dimension to our lives.

Swamping our senses

The human body presents us with a constant flood of experiences from our very real physical challenges. Our brain manages every aspect of our physical being except our spiritual feelings. Our brain memory areas record our experiences, assimilating some of the information we try to take in and our learning curves. In short, our physical being swamps our senses and almost every moment is focused on our physical activities, our work and education, our relationships, actions and worries. There has never been a time in human history when we have grounded ourself so much in television, computers, smart phones, social media and entertainment. Many people don't allow themselves a time of quiet meditation. Our spiritual feelings often cannot be made sense of, so we may not prioritise them.

Our brain is our link with the physical world

 When a person suffers with Alzheimer's or Dementia the brain sustains damage, often affecting the short-term memory. Subsequently it may change a person's character and make them unable to take care of personal needs. I have given many clairvoyant readings where I connect with a loved one ultimately passed primarily due to such illness. In every single case the person in spirit had given me messages that prove beyond doubt that they are restored to the personality before the onset of brain disease. Usually, their memories are intact but stop at the point in life of the onset of their illness. Loved ones who I am offering the reading to are usually amazed at the contact with their loved one who has the personality and memories from their healthier years. As with every mediumship reading, I have given over many years, the soul in Spirit always retains their memories and their character. This has provided overwhelming evidence that our soul energy retains a full data bank of memories and that our character is truly a reflection of our soul being.

Our brain retains memories, with different areas of the brain for both long and short-term memories. The brain tends to retain more technical information than the soul memory such as telephone numbers.
Recent research has shown an increase in activity of the memory areas of brain when a person is dying. This discovery was by accident when medical teams were monitoring brain activity for someone seriously ill whom they didn't expect to die. They witnessed much of the brain dying, except the memory areas increased their activity.
The idea of our brain uploading our memories to our soul is not new. Many people who have experienced a drowning incident but were saved describe their "Whole life flashing before them" in almost an instant.

Losing awareness of our soul and the spiritual realm often intensifies people's hurtful behavior. Our brain holds no memories of our spiritual existence before our birth, so it is understandable if people make comments such as "I don't believe in anything spiritual". When people say this to me, I believe they are entitled to their beliefs and make no comment. Their outlook and beliefs are how we are almost programmed to respond by the Higher Creative Power that placed our soul into life as a human being.

Question: *"Why can't I remember any existence before my life began?"*

"You are a soul energy that is connected to your body through your brain in such a way that you feel as one with your physical body. This union of soul to brain is so perfect that many people feel that all they are is their physical body. At birth your soul merges with the brain of a newborn baby. Your soul memory is supressed as it merges with a newly created physical brain that has no memories. So, you temporarily lose your conscious memories of Heaven. Your soul memories of Heaven and previous existence are now confined to your super conscious memory. Your soul memories are restored at the end of physical life".

Question: *"How do we truly know that we are spiritual, that we have a soul?"*

"A soul feels emotions. True, the brain generates physical emotional reactions such a laughter and tears, but the soul sends messages to the brain first. The soul expresses itself in music, art, the need for adventure. If people were nothing more than a human computer then there would be no need for such things, and no need for emotions".

CHAPTER TWO:

Personal Spiritual Qualities

Q uestion: "I really care about people but often feel totally drained when trying to help them by listening to their problems."
Answer: "There are many souls who only talk about themselves. These souls are immature and show little care for others. They attract sympathy because their life situation might be one of many things going wrong. This can be lack of money, poor health, poor living conditions, broken relationships, misfortune. Yes, you might show care, but take care to protect your spiritual energies because such people can be energy vampires. After a period listening to them and showing care you might feel spiritually drained, whereas they have stolen some of your energies and feel better. They usually only feel better for a short while. Make a quiet inner prayer to God to protect your energies, your spiritual integrity, and pull away if you realise that your spiritual energies are being drained."

Question: "Does love for others seem to be too soft in this world of challenges, fighting and greed?"

Answer: "Love has to be "Tough Love" because God's love is tough love. Souls are given life as human beings that will have challenges. If God's love were soft our lives would be easy and a utopian paradise. However, souls only learn, only progress in spiritual development when faced with challenges. If a person can overcome difficulties and challenges and yet retain the ability to love they will have spiritually grown."

Question: "Why is life so hard. Doesn't Heaven see the suffering in this world?"

Answer: "Life may seem incredibly tough and cruel at times, especially for most people in modern society who are not given true spiritual knowledge and understanding. Imagine a young person who has lived at home in a seaside town. His parents might tell him he must go out to sea on a boat or ship to catch fish and earn a living. He will meet many challenges and risk his life. Heaven is the safe place like the family home in the seaside town. Life as a human being is like the journey on the sea. There might be storms where every part of our being struggles to survive, contrasted by periods of sunshine and calm. Heaven knows that it is the safe, loving home that all souls can return to. However, the experience of human beings in life can sometimes be too cruel and too painful. God's love really can be tough love."

Question: *"What is Love?"*

Answer: "In Heaven love is the energy that surrounds us. We can feel the gentle warmth and security of unconditional love. On Earth, in life as human beings we may or may not find love from our mother or father. As we grow into adulthood, we may seek love in a close friend or partner. Often attraction is confused with love, but they are not the same. When we have no love in our lives, we may feel insular and create an invisible wall to protect our feelings and emotions. Animals who we keep as pets such as a dog can show unconditional love if we care for them."

Question: *"Is it good to stop in our busy lives?"*

Answer: "The Angels encourage people to stop in their busy life and feel the spiritual realities of beauty and peace. Making time to stop is captured in the following Affirmation."

In Stillness
In stillness, look at a beautiful flower,
A bloom of colour, and fragrance,
Nature's finest hour

In stillness, gaze at night-time sky,
The stars, the universe,
And wonder why.

In stillness, let spirit wander free,
Sense the love of God,
True reality.

In stillness, and peace,
Inwardly pray,
For strength and guidance
On life's difficult way.

In stillness you may find
That time matters not,
Timeless peace rediscovered,
Perhaps almost forgot.

Question: *"Are our physical senses limited in perception of a true reality?"*

Answer: "The Angels teach us to look at the world from a different perspective to help our understanding of the meaning of life."

Our physical senses are limited and few,
There are things we can discover,
If the truth, we knew.

We cannot see, touch, hear, smell or taste gravity,
Yet, we can perceive,
Perhaps the strongest force in the universe
Science teaches, we believe.

We cannot see, touch, hear, smell or taste radio, everywhere,
Carrying unseen messages through the atmosphere.

We cannot see, touch, hear, smell or taste our soul,
Science denies our soul is real,
Yet, our soul energy manifests in all human expression, emotion, how we feel,
This most important evidence science has missed.

Question: *"As eternal souls are we connected to each other somehow?"*

Answer: "All souls are connected. They are part of a oneness of soul that exists in the spiritual realm of Heaven."

Oneness of Soul
Our soul energy is a conscious energy,
It is all of whom we are within
Deep inside it is the "I" or "Me",
We may feel like the only "One.
We are all connected to a spiritual Oneness,
In Heaven of the Spiritual dimension
Our true, familiar home,
Of conscious energy, love, and creation.

Unity of Soul
If we cause hurt or harm to someone,
Or to any living thing that has a soul

We are really hurting a part of ourselves,
As some might say "Scoring an own goal"
...against ourselves.

Question: I feel lacking in fulfilment. Why?

Answer: "All souls have a Life Plan that was determined in Heaven before birth. A Life Plan is meant to have challenges and positive experiences that bring fulfilment. If people take notice of their intuitive feelings, they are tuning in to guidance from their Guardian Angels who know their Life Plan. Think of visions you may have in your mind about something you want to do or achieve. Try your best to work towards the visions and your Angels will help you by bringing guidance every day into your intuitive feelings. Life Fulfilment doesn't have to be money or physical possessions. "

The Angels teach me that the most important spiritual quality is to be caring to others, to animals and nature.

A Person Who Cares
"Please find me food, I'm hungry,
Please give me water I'm dry,
Don't leave me, don't ignore me,
Or I will surely die"
"You are a stranger here amongst us,
In this war-torn famine land
Please show me that you care,
Show me you understand"

The stranger stopped and said, "You're suffering I understand",
"I will lead you away from here,
Come, please take my hand,
To a place of food abundant
Where water freely flows

To a land of peace and freedom
Where children learn and grow"

The suffering all followed this stranger,
Her goodness they all knew,
Are you a caring person?
Could this stranger, perhaps, be you?

I am shown by the Angels that in Heaven everyone is equally important, no matter what our position was in life. Their message is captured in the following Affirmation.

Just a Number
To the world I'm just a number,
Along with all the rest,
Never getting anywhere or earning much,
Although I always keep trying my best
I know I'll never be famous,
And wealth never comes my way,
What little I earn goes on food and home,
As I struggle through each day.
So, what colour is there in my life?
I ask myself many times,
The same work and routines every day
Are the usual experience of mine.
Yet what of the rich and famous
With their houses and property Fine?
For a person can only make use of
One room and one chair at a time
We are all breathing same air as each other,
And however, our friendships are sought,
The best and truest of friends
Can never, ever be bought.
A scenic view and the beauty of nature
Are things that we all can see,

And the experience of sport, art, and music
Can cost little, and often found free.
So, when I think of myself as a number,
It's only an emotional test,
The truth is we all are important,
Yes, you and I are as good as the Best!

I have given many thousands of people Angel messages concerning a soul of a loved one, now in Heaven. On every occasion the Angels show me that souls in Heaven have their memories and the same character.

<u>Memories</u>
Days of old, days of gold,
My memories are as autumn shades.
Life was "Nothing special" at the time,
But looking back I can now define,
Those special moments that stand out
With a warmth and fondness that removes all doubt
That the "Nothing special" was important to me
In this life that to others seems so ordinary.

Through my research I have discovered that our person Angel companions are with us much of the time. We are viewed with respect and loved unconditionally. Life is a gift for our soul to have adventure and experience and importantly, learn. It is deliberate that we can't see Angels or hear them speak to us.
The Angels from Heaven work in unconditional love and only ever bring positive, helpful messages. They communicate through our feelings, our intuition and our conscience. We will never, or rarely hear a voice in our mind. We can learn how to recognise messages from the Angels, and I describe how this works in the following narrative "Aspects of the Soul":

ASPECTS OF THE SOUL
The term "Aspects of the Soul" is used in spiritual communities in many different ways. It can mean the three Aspects of Mind, Body and

Spirit. It can be the ancient Egyptian belief of the soul having different parts. I see all human souls as an energy that is just "One". Within the "One" we create our own areas in which our soul may resonate. These vary from person to person, and can be many areas, but I broadly categorise these into the Aspects of Higher Self, Middle Self, and Lower Self.

Aspects of the Soul-Middle Self
Like an unseen wind that blows to who knows where
Our invisible soul energy, is whom we are, always there,
As a gentle breeze on a fine summer day
Our soul may be gentle and full of play,
Storms come in our lives and our souls energise,
As destructive winds in a storm, are our actions ever wise?

Our souls have three aspects, Higher, Middle, Low
In which our soul resonates, in these poems I will show.
Most of life's time our soul resonates in self-centre,
The middle level of our existence we most often enter

Self-centred is normal for food, shelter, money,
Entertainment, life journeys, stressful or funny

Materialistic world adverts target us every day,
To buy more desires, phone, car, holiday,
Shop for leisure, shop for pleasure,
Spend, spend every day,
In Middle Self we are grounded,
our very being might go astray,
We may not feel our Guardian Angels,
Many in this world lose their way.

Aspects of the Soul - Lower Self

Many souls resonate at times in lower self,
Primitive, worse than animal, greed, seeking power, and wealth
They never put their thoughts in other people's place,
Cold hearts destroy lives, a scourge on the human race.

Psychological bullies, cause physical hurt, pain, and fear,
Steal energies from those around, family, friends, and others near

Living each day in Lower Self, Guardian Angels cannot get through,
To live like that is a free will choice,
Negative energy may take over you,
And leave you devoid of love, hurting others on the way,
Precious lives destroyed by self-centred people every day.

Aspects of the Soul - Higher Self
A caring, loving soul may lift-up to Higher Self,
Needs of others before themselves, not concerned with Wealth
They have a secret, I will share, for tired they often may be,
When helping others they feel stronger
Their soul feels more energy,
…………..From the Angels

In Higher Self, unconditional love,
Is a perfect energy,
Our Angels connect more closely, setting our soul free,
………….. of Life's burden's

Our Life Plan will be clearer,
For our Angels already know,
They hold a vision of our future,
Whom we'll meet, and where we'll go

Guardian Angels speak through our feelings,

Intuitive knowing of what's wrong and right,
Ways forward through our problems
Our life now filled with Light

In Middle Self, and Lower self, our Angels are still there,
We may not know their presence,
Until we resonate in love, and care,
……... for others.

Become more loving, and more caring,
Qualities of spiritual strength, and grace,
Let us learn, let us grow,
We can make the world a better place.

The wonderful, amazing, and profound impact on our lives of becoming closer to our Guardian Angels and discovering the Angels that are there to help each one of us can be life changing!

A "CALLING"

Ever wondered why some people are so determined to do something to help others? Why some people are determined to work helping animals, nature, or the environment?
I believe that many people are given a "Calling". This is a gift from Heaven to do a particular task. The task is part of a Divine Plan to make sure that every aspect of life has people interested in caring and working to cherish, protect, repair, and bring healing
Our Guardian Angels know this Divine Plan and work to help those with a Calling to help them fulfil their inner driving force to care for other people, or care for animals, nature, and planet Earth.

A Calling

Someone called my name – no-one there,
I heard it again – from where?
Perhaps imagination, yet, inner-feelings, new sensation
Heightened awareness, inspiration.
I must help others, I must show care,

New ideas in my mind, guiding me – where?
Yes, I now see it clearly, people suffering out there.

I know it won't be a perfect way,
Somehow, I'll help others each day,
No longer thinking just about me,
Money, pleasure, living selfishly.

A new driving force, like fire within,
I must get started, I must begin,
Trying to help others, new goals in sight,
It matters more that I try,
Than to always get it right.

Touching lives, kindness, goodness, share,
Giving, helping,
My new purpose is to care.

*Do we spend money on too many physical goods, polluting the planet,
or do we focus our efforts on climate change prevention?*

Money
When I think about money,
Food, clothing, home costs, are a problem sometimes,
And I need a little money for extra things,
The interests and pleasures of mine.

I often wish I had more money, my income a bigger share,
I could buy things I've always wanted, travel anywhere.

Yet, when I think of what I care for most, remind myself I try,
True friends, family, the beauty of nature,
Money just can't buy.

CHAPTER THREE

Angels and Guardian Angels

W ho or What are Angels?
Heaven is another dimension. This isn't anything to fear because it is our true home. Our soul energy is made of the same energies as Heaven. Our life in the physical form as human beings has always been nothing more than a temporary home with joy and love contrasted by times of unhappiness and fear.

I don't always see Angels having wings. I perceive that visions of Angels in modern or ancient times would be in their true radiance. They radiate spiritual energies that appear as light. The visual effect of radiating light is easily understood. Spiritual energies that are breaking through from another dimension are not affected by gravity. An Angelic Being appearing as a vision will most likely appear somehow suspended in the air. To ancient people, the only way that any living thing could appear in the air is if, like a bird, they had wings to fly. Hence. Angels with their beautiful, radiating, shimmering light were described by witnesses as having wings so they could fly.

I don't know who or what are all of the Beings in Heaven. As a human being, even with the gift of clairvoyance, we can only glimpse some of Heaven from our position in life.

I will describe what I know.

There are Angels who are purely spiritual of spiritual existence and there are Angels who were once people. The Angels that were once people have lived many human lives and judged to be sufficiently advanced and experienced to become a Guardian Angel. They would typically accompany one or more people in life and try to guide and help them as necessary. Some might be good at bringing healing or they might seek the help of healing Angels. Some cultures, in particular the American Indians, call them "Spirit Guides". This term has been picked up by many in the clairvoyant community, but I prefer the term "Guardian Angel".

I have also no doubt that many spiritual beings are dedicated to maintaining life in nature.

The support for ourselves and for life in nature brings to our realisation that there are truly billions of Angels. The support from Heaven for ourselves and life is so vast as to be almost beyond our imagination. What awareness of this is held by billions of people? Astonishingly, very little awareness. Self-centred people constantly fight each other for power, control, for assets that they can acquire and own without realising that they are totally oblivious to the spiritual realm.

I cannot emphasise enough how Heaven views all souls as being equal. There are Archangels as my very real spiritual experience describes. Archangels are closer to the purpose of the Source of whom religions may name "God".

Beyond the Archangels there are Wise Beings who have the authority to judge our soul's progress in our recent life. I am not able to say how they judge, but spiritual progress is acquired by being genuinely loving and caring in actions towards other people, and towards animals, nature and the environment. Spiritual regression is when a soul has caused hurt to others and nature. All people in life make many mistakes and we are forgiven for times when we caused hurt. It helps heal the situation if we genuinely feel aware of the hurt that we caused and are aware of our wrongdoings.

There are many people in life that hurt others and nature because they don't care. They are unaware of the fact that there will have to face a spiritual review of their life in Heaven.

Question: "Are there different kinds of Angels?"

Answer: "There are many different types of Angelic beings in the dimension of Heaven. We can describe many of them as Angels, and Guardian Angels. Guardian Angels are with each of us personally throughout life. There are healing Angels to channel healing energies to people, and to animals and nature. There are Archangels and other spiritual beings who work in the Spiritual Realm to support Creation. You can look-up the term "Angel" which is translated as "Messenger of God".

Question: "I see Angels, and wonder how I can help others see them?"

Answer: "Try reciting the following Visualisation to someone who is truly wanting to see an Angel. You know that visions in your mind can be drawn from memory or can be given to you spiritually".

Visualisation to see your Guardian Angel
Imagine yourself in a dark room,
Feel safe and secure, can't see in dark gloom.

A door starts to open, brightness behind,
Your room fills with light, gently you find,
Yourself lifting and moving out to the light,
That surrounds and bathes you, all now feels right.

Yet still nothing to see in this bright gentle mist,
Feel heightened awareness, what will you see first?

The mist starts to clear, appears a garden fine,
Just like a Spring morning, air sweet as wine,
Flowers of red, yellow, white, intense, a sign

ROBERT MASON

To one standing before you, a Being Divine

Your Guardian Angel radiant, eyes now meet yours,
Already knows you, love, forgiving your flaws,
Angel understands, loved for whom you are,
Love unconditional, Heaven is not far.

Your soul uplifted, this place 'tween Heaven and Earth,
A place you last visited just before your birth.

Time now to return, feel cleansed, uplifted, still,
Henceforth, to just know your Guardian Angel will,
Always be with you.

Guardian Angels are real, but elusive. They try not to give the game away that
many of them were once people.

Guardian Angels
Who or what are Guardian Angels?
Some are as people,
Who have lived through many lives,
Are spiritually grown, now sufficiently wise,
to guide us in our lives

Their soul energy is pure and wonderful,
No matter how and when
Spiritual beings so beautiful
Yet we are important to them.

They bring the unconditional love of Heaven,
They know our inner being,
Our good and bad, mistakes,
Forgiveness isn't needed,
For their compassion and understanding is absolute

CHAPTER FOUR

What is the purpose of life?

Question to Heaven: "What is the purpose of life?"

Answer: *"The reasons for giving souls a life as a human being are many. One of the main reasons is for the Experience,"*

EXPERIENCE
One purpose of life is experience,
For its experience that we seek,
In our work, interests and travel,
reading, or with others speak.
Too much of the same experience,
is when we may start to get bored,
As can happen in daily routine,
You know, those everyday chores. One purpose of life seems quite simple,

the need for experience drives our soul,
From birth to old age, through the years of our life,
towards an ultimate goal.

So, one purpose of life is experience,
part of life's mystery revealed anew,
When bored with your life, seek fulfilment,
Find something new and interesting to do!

The Path of Life

Through life I travelled every day,
Somewhere, I took the wrong path, on my way,
Hostile people stopped me, wanting fight,
The fight had no winners, no wrong or right,
Fighting ended because I showed care,
People now accepted me, friendship to share.
 I travelled again on this unknown path,
Hunger and thirst, no rod, no staff.
 I came across food, replenished my supply,
A voice in the distance for food did cry,
I tried to ignore them, my food was my own,
I turned back to help; I had spiritually grown.

I fed the poor stranger, offered my hand,
To a place on the path, food abundance land
I moved on, my search, emptiness inside,
A search for love to heal pain, deep down I did hide,
Path went over mountains, heat and cold,
My clothes were but rags, I felt weary, old,
In search of greater meaning, fulfilment, and truth,
Inner happiness I hadn't found whilst in my youth.
I travelled further on this path, rounded a bend,
My path went two ways to journey's end,
The first was for learning, hard lessons I'd seen,
The second, now open, almost a dream,
I took this second path, better in deeds and thought,
Now caring for others, from lessons life had taught,
Then I saw a Light ahead, as I rested by a tree,
My beautiful Guardian Angel waiting all along for me.

CHAPTER FIVE

God, Jesus, Holy Scripture

Question: "Is there a God?"

Answer: "In Heaven souls can sense and feel a power watching over them. God is a Oneness, and all souls feel that connection. Heaven is a place where love is a real tangible energy. God is the eternal spiritual creative intelligence and purpose of everything. The soul journey is to learn and progress through many lives, and eventually through further learning experiences to re-unite with God.

Question: *"Is Jesus Christ real?"*

Answer: "Absolutely Yes. Following the teachings of Christ in the way people live their life is what Heaven expects. However, Jesus Christ did not want Churches to differ from each other, disagree or fight. Jesus Christ did not want people to fear that they might not survive death and reach Heaven. Most souls reach Heaven without religious faith because God loves everyone. Souls are more certain to reach a better place in Heaven living according to Holy Scripture."

Question: "Holy Scripture teaches forgiveness. Is that sometimes being too soft on the perpetrator?"

Answer. "Forgiveness doesn't mean allowing the perpetrator to get away with harmful behaviour. Firstly, God is the judge. In Heaven all serious wrongdoings will be addressed. Secondly, the legal justice system may give a perpetrator a criminal punishment. Countries may wage war to confront nations driven by the devil. On a personal basis forgiveness means not taking revenge.

Question: "What does Heaven think about anger?"

Answer: "If you are angry with someone you hurt inside. You may suffer the emotional pain of anger. Try to let anger go. The hurt inside caused by anger is probably not being felt by the perpetrator so they are winning as long as you hurt with anger. Try to assess the situation cooly with little emotion. Do not allow them to keep hurting you. Walk away if possible."

Question to Heaven: "Does Heaven give us spiritual signs?"

Answer: "Yes, we often give signs such as a bird coming unusually close, or a butterfly".

The Dove
A hundred doves swept o'er the sky,
White, innocent beauty, they did fly,
and circled back, I knew not why,
Rising, falling, before my eye,
A oneness, yes, a oneness, I couldn't deny.
One dove broke away, glided down to me near
Wanting to be close, no wild bird fear.

This single dove, was of all doves ever,

as if the only one,
In its beauty, oneness of every dove,
since Creation, time begun.

A message came across that when we pray,
A part of Heaven's Oneness may come our way,
A fleeting moment to worship,
that our lives be blessed,
To pray for hopes, needs,
and ask forgiveness.

CHAPTER SIX

Personal proof of an Afterlife

Question: *"What are Near-Death Experiences (NDE's)?"*

Answer: "Science tells us that there is currently no proof of our soul and Heaven. The most common ways that human beings can accept that there is a spiritual dimension and that we ourselves have a soul are through either religious beliefs or personal spiritual experiences. In modern times so called "Near Death Experiences" have become widely recorded. This is because many people who have been near death due to injury or serious illness have been saved by modern day professional medical help. During their time at the closest point to death some estimates indicate that around 17% of people experience an out-of-body spiritual event that can be recalled later. These NDE experiences can be totally convincing and life changing. Sometimes those experiencing an NDE can recall seeing their Guardian Angel.

The following is a true account of a Near Death Experience:

Peter was proud of his motor bike and travelled everywhere on it, including travel to work. Kate, his girlfriend constantly worried about him riding his bike because he seemed oblivious to danger, especially in bad weather situations. The day that he had his accident was a weekend and he decided to visit his parents who lived nine miles away from his home. The weather was quite bad with heavy rain and strong winds as he travelled on a country road out of town. His bike suddenly hit a bump in the road that knocked his steering. The bike started to swerve uncontrollably on the wet road surface. He came off the road and hit a tree and everything went black.

Peter found himself awake in hospital. He was looking down at a hospital bed with a doctor and two nurses attending someone who was unconscious. It took him a moment to realise that the person they were attending was himself. He didn't feel concerned, nor did he feel afraid. He felt good and yet he knew what the doctor and nurses were thinking. The nurses were thinking "He won't make it. He is going to die". The doctor was thinking "I will try my best to save him".

Peter found himself being drawn to a light at the side of the room. The light seemed warm and inviting as he entered its loving embrace. He was moving at high speed in what seemed like a tunnel at the end of which was the source of the light. He could see the vague outline of two people stood in the light. Suddenly he found himself in a calm, beautiful meadow. The grass was green, and flowers of every shade seemed to shine with a vivid intensity that left him lost for words. Peter was surprised at how he felt. All his senses were working yet he had no physical body. His soul energy was his body. He felt as though this was the true reality of home. Unconditional love was around him like the air that he had breathed in life. Peter also experienced a profound feeling of oneness with the universe.

He was met by his grandma who he knew had died last year. His grandad was stood with her. He had died nine years earlier. "It is not your time," said his grandma. Peter felt totally unconcerned about the life he had just left. "Can I stay here?" said Peter. His grandma did not reply as a spiritual being appeared in the form of person but radiating light and he felt that this was an Angel. The Angel had no wings and appeared with white and purple radiant garments and a presence that felt loving but strict, with some spiritual authority. "You have things to do that we planned for you in your life. You must go back", said the Angel. "Are you, my Guardian Angel?" asked Peter. Before he received a response, he suddenly felt himself much heavier and began to feel some discomfort and pain. He opened his eyes and realised that he was back in his body in a hospital bed. A nurse saw that he had regained consciousness and he heard her say to a colleague "He is awake, thank goodness, I thought we had lost him".

Peter eventually made a full recovery although he never rode a motor bike again. He was reluctant to tell people about his NDE, but he did tell his girlfriend Kate. Kate was the person who told me about this when she came to me for Angel messages. During the consultation I was given a message that her boyfriend had been injured in a motor incident and that it had changed his life. She confirmed to me that Peter had experienced this life changing event and that it had made him more caring towards her and others. Peter was no longer scared at the thought of death, but now knew that it was only the beginning of another stage in the eternal life of his true inner being.

The following is a further true account of a NDE, but a different experience:

Alison was on holiday with her sister at a popular seaside holiday resort on the south coast of England. The weather was hot and sunny, so they headed for the beach. There were lifeguard stations so the two felt totally at ease as they walked into the sea. "I'll race you swimming up to that buoy" said her sister Carol. The buoy floated bright orange about two hundred yards off the beach. It was probably something securing a fishing pot for catching lobsters or crabs. Alison reached the buoy first and turned to see Carol approaching her and looking frustrated because she came second. The girls, both aged in their twenties, held position together at the buoy. "The water is cold!" shouted Alison. "Come on let's get back to the beach and warm up in the sun". "You go first" she said to Carol. "I will still try to win".

Carol lunged forward to swim towards the beach in the cold sea water. Alison waited a few seconds then struck forward to swim back. Suddenly her arms and legs went into severe cramp. The shock of the cold sea was hitting her. She struggled to keep swimming but the harder she tried the more her arms and legs screamed with pain. She could no longer swim and found herself being submerged. She tried to get her head above water and screamed for help. The cold sea started to swallow her. It seemed quite deep and small waves that she hadn't really noticed were hindering her attempts to gasp a mouthful of air. She realised she was drowning and going under. Her senses of panic overwhelmed her. In her mind her life flashed before her. Every minute of her life could be vividly seen, ending in her sadness at the memory of her daughter, now aged two years, at home with her partner Mike who was at home while she took a day out with her sister.

The pain in her limbs disappeared and then she felt herself in a place of blackness. She couldn't understand what has happened to her but didn't feel frightened. A small light appeared in the distance, racing towards her and getting bigger as it approached. The light quickly reached her, and she felt at ease and surrounded by light. The light enveloped like a warm blanket of love as she saw in the light an Angel and her father who had died the previous year. The Angel looked on with love as her father gave her a message: "It's not your time Alison. Tell your mother I love her and that I still watch over her". Another beautiful Angel then came into view. Without words she knew it was her Guardian Angel who knew everything about her, her good and bad, and loved her unconditionally for whom she was and is.

The moment on the edge of Heaven came to and ended as she awoke coughing up sea water, gasping for breath. She felt cold like she had never been before, and her breathing was painful. She was alive. The lifeguards had been quick to act when they heard her screams before she went under the water. Carol was with her and held her hand as she was taken by stretcher into an ambulance and then on to the local A&E hospital.

After an overnight stay in hospital Alison made a full recovery.

Many months later she came to see me for Angel messages. Her father came through and her Guardian Angel brought through a vision of this incident that Alison confirmed as correct. Her life had been changed forever by her near-death experience and she felt spiritually stronger. Alison was happy and deeply moved emotionally to hear messages from her father.

As with most people who have experienced an NDE she now seemed to value every moment of every day as a blessing and life as a precious gift. Her experience of life flashing before her eyes as she was drowning has led to questions in my spiritual research. This is quite a common experience.

Some people have experienced Near Death Experiences "NDE's". For others a strong feeling of their spirituality that often cannot be explained helps them seek to learn more concerning the meaning of life and spiritual self-discovery.

The following is a true account of a NDE:

Dave, aged in his early twenties, was driving his car home on a main road early one December evening. His car was in a long line of traffic at a steady speed of around fifty miles per hour. Suddenly he saw the headlights of a vehicle travelling in the opposite direction veer across the towards him. He had no chance to avoid a head on collision. The driver of the other vehicle had suffered a heart attack at the wheel and died instantly. The collision was head on between the vehicles, with a combined impact speed of around one hundred miles per hour.

Dave found himself conscious and looking down on the scene of the accident. He could see people trying to tend to the injured and noticed that he was one of them, trapped in his car, unconscious. He felt no panic as he seemed to feel detached from the real situation as if it were a video film. Then all went black. He awoke in hospital, but again looking down on himself in a hospital bed, and his body was unconscious. However, he felt alive and well as his soul hovered from a position overhead at ceiling height. He could sense the thoughts of two nurses who were attending him and that they thought he was going to die. Dave noticed a light in the corner of the room at ceiling height. It was incredibly bright, and he sensed it was a portal to Heaven. He knew that if he entered the light his physical life would end. So, he resisted and kept telling himself "No way am I ready to die just yet". At that moment a doctor entered the room and Dave could sense the thoughts of the doctor "I will save him". He saw the doctor inject him with some medication and then all went black. He awoke later and felt the pain of his injuries. He was still alive. Dave has since made a full recovery, yet his spiritual experience changed him forever. He now knows that we all survive physical death, and that there is a much longer journey for our soul beyond this life. Furthermore, he had retained his character and memories whilst in his out of body state."

Question: "Can I tell people how I first experienced a vision of Heaven?"

Answer: "Your proof of Heaven was through a spiritual experience of an Archangel that changed your life forever. You captured this experience in the poem that you wrote shortly after. Publish this for others to read".

The Archangel
The first of May, nineteen ninety-nine,
an Archangel appeared before me, Divine
Spring morning, sun shining, air sweet as wine,
Yet the beauty and radiance before me a sign...from Heaven

I bowed down in fear, but fear did not last
Archangel before me, from Holy Scriptures past,
His flowing robes, radiant, shone so bright as I saw,
A face of understanding, a moment beyond awe.
I was drawn to His eyes, full of love I was seeing,
He knew who I was, knew my life, knew my being,
Unconditional love, and forgiveness for mistakes I was feeling,

"Come with me" was the message, and I swiftly did rise

A path of light from Heaven, then to my surprise,
Into view came a place of landscape, beauty, so real
Green valleys, trees, flowers, vivid colours, I could feel
The air that I breathed was unconditional love,
All around me, surrounding, and a sense of Higher Heavens above.

"This is "First Heaven", Archangel did say,
"A place of rest for souls when they leave life's day"
I could see people in joy, as they danced in this place,
Where all good souls enter from our human race
There were houses and gardens, and white buildings too
A library in Heaven holding a book of life for you.

Archangel, radiant, up again we did rise
To a Higher Heaven of cloud, and to my surprise,
Angels were working, planning and healing life
Helping those on Earth through adventures and strife.
The Angels nearby turned towards me and smiled,
They bowed down to Archangel, and I stopped for a while.

Above me a Light of Third Heaven of our Creator
The Source of all Purpose, God of Love, and our Saviour.

"It is time to return," Archangel did say,
"I have a purpose for you, to help others each day",
"The Angels will bring visions and messages to you,
For those in grief from bereavement, so you can help them through",
"Another gift will be healing, though your body be weak,
The Angels will channel healing for those who seek",
"A gift of seeing the First Heaven, whenever you need,
A gift of knowledge of Life's meaning
The Universe, the Seed...Of Life"

I suddenly was back, my feet on the ground,
Archangel was gone,
No-one near but the sound
Of a perfect Spring morning,

Birds singing around,
...With the joy of Life.

CHAPTER SEVEN

Clairvoyant readings are
messages from the Angels

I have helped many thousands of people suffering bereavement grief in a way that is hard to find elsewhere. I know that the unconditional love of God is with me through the Guardian Angels that help me in this work...........

Mediumship Readings
Mediumship readings can be performed anytime, anywhere by a clairvoyant and a willing client. They almost always offer significant evidence of the survival of the human soul beyond physical death.
The following true account is interesting in the way that a life can be dramatically changed by spiritually analysing a person's life in recent years to bring about a much brighter and positive future:
I was called to a home in Hull to give several readings, to a bunch of family and friends who had booked me. Halfway through the evening I was invited into a room to read for a lady in her late sixties. I had met these friends gathered in the lounge, and then one at a time walked through to the kitchen/diner to give each a private reading. The room this lady was sat in was in between the lounge and kitchen. It was reasonably big, decorated in the flowery wallpaper so popular in the 1970s. This was the year 2006. I noticed that there was no window in the room, but it was bright and clean. She looked happy, but as I started to give her a reading, I felt very much that her life was on hold. I immediately saw a man with her in spirit who I knew was her husband. I told

her this, she nodded to confirm, when I was then given a picture of a scene of a hospital bed. The same man was laid there with full life support systems attached. A doctor was in this scene looking past me at the lady I was with, asking her permission to switch off the life support. The doctor was telling her that there was nothing more the medical professionals could do. Her husband was technically brain dead, but his body was being kept alive by the machines. I gently told the lady what I was seeing. She remained calm and told me that her husband had died six years earlier. The doctor had indeed asked her permission to switch off the life support. She couldn't say yes, so went for a walk around the local streets. She had then walked back into the ward still unable to bring herself to give permission. Suddenly she just came out with the words necessary, giving permission for the life support to be switched off. The lady had remained calm whilst she told me all of this. She then became quite emotional, and said, "I murdered him. I murdered him. I have locked myself away in this room for the past six years. I haven't been out. I am looked after by my family, but I won't go out. I killed my husband." Her emotional outburst shocked me, but only momentarily. I was instantly taken back to the hospital ward. I had a bird's-eye view of her returning after her walk. I could see and hear her asking for the doctor, still undecided what to do, when suddenly her husband appeared, stood alongside her in spirit whispering in her ear "Switch off the life support. I am ok, I am free of my wrecked body, please tell him you give your permission, my love". The vision disappeared and I sat facing this emotionally distraught lady sat in front of me. I told her what I had just seen. I told her that her husband had not really been lying there in the hospital bed but was stood alongside her in spirit asking her to tell the doctor to switch off the life support.

The clairvoyant visions closed as I sat opposite this lady. She slowly lifted her drooping head and stared at me eye to eye. Then a smile appeared. "You couldn't have known all of this. I now believe that my husband still exists. I did the right thing. I made the right decision."

I was then ushered out of her room to give another reading in the kitchen to a friend who had been waiting. At the end of the evening, I walked into the lounge to say goodbye to everyone. The air of excitement was electrifying. A middle-aged lady who must have been the daughter said, "Mum has told us she is no longer grieving, she is no longer blaming herself for Dad's death. She wants to get her life going again. Her first request is that I take her out shopping tomorrow. Thank you for what you have done. You have no idea what a miracle it is to see Mum wanting to live her life again." I said goodnight, feeling very much that something much bigger than me was at work. I can't perform miracles but overwhelmingly felt humbled to be a part of something so life changing.

The following is a true account of a psychic reading that involved seeing the future for a lady. Without her telling me anything beforehand, I discovered in the reading that her family were deeply troubled by what had happened to their son. During the reading I saw two outcomes for their son, one good, and one not so good, so I focussed on the good path, and the future changed as I spoke to become the better outcome.

The lady sitting in front of me screamed. Her scream shook the house and surely neighbours would come running in to see what had happened. I was a stranger who had been sat facing this lady across a kitchen table for no more than five minutes. Her scream shook me with an unexpected shudder of sudden stress because I am not the kind of guy who does anything to make women scream! I am a clairvoyant and she had booked me to visit her home to give her a reading. This lady was aged around forty years and was obviously taking no care of her appearance with greasy hair all over the place, and scruffy clothes. She seemed depressed as she welcomed me into her house and sat me down.

My first words were simply "It's about Justice – or rather an injustice – your son is in prison for an offence he didn't commit" That is when she screamed. I'd visualised some heavy weight fighter of a husband appearing and throwing me out - but fortunately she had kicked him out of the house for a few hours for privacy during the reading. What I told her was correct, but then I went on to tell her that her son's prison sentence would be overturned, and he would be a free man within four weeks. Her scream was of surprise at how I could possibly know all of this. I spent another hour with her, bringing-in some quite clear messages from her deceased mother. She calmed down very quickly and became more optimistic and much happier over that hour, and the messages from her mum appeared to be of great meaning. I left her with good wishes, inside my mind saying a quiet prayer for her and her son.

This was in the city of Hull, which I only visit several times a year, and I never go to the public houses there. However, about a month later I did call into a Hull pub with some friends, but in a different area of the city. Hull is a big place. Within minutes an attractive lady came running up to me and gave me a big hug saying: "Its him… its him…". I couldn't help but notice a rather tough looking partner behind her looking quite angry at her behaviour. "It's ok" she told him "This is the clairvoyant". The partner changed his mood, put a smile on his face and shook my hand "Our son is no longer in prison, everything you said came true". The fact that their son was now free was good news, but the added miracle for me was the transformation of this lady. She had taken on a new zest for living, pulled herself out of depression, and acquired a new interest in taking care of herself. She had given herself a makeover with her hair and dress, with such a dramatic improvement that I didn't recognise her immediately. This was the miracle of what clairvoyance can offer. I have witnessed this miracle many times as people take their lives off "hold" and start living again. My friends in the pub had been staring- on in amazement. I didn't openly discuss my clairvoyant work. One of my hobbies is singing, and we had just done a concert, so my fellow singers in the pub knew nothing about my clairvoyance work. I just tried to shoulder-off what had happened in a joking way.

CHAPTER EIGHT

What is Heaven Like?

"There are many places in Heaven. Most souls reach a place called First Heaven. This is a place of orientation where a soul can meet loved ones who have passed, and rest to recharge their soul energies. First Heaven is quite Earth-like in appearance. There are beautiful gardens, valleys, trees. There are houses and physical objects that help us feel that we are in familiar surroundings. Souls may rest or keep busy because there is much to do. Souls may even be reunited with a pet that we cared for such as a dog, cat, or horse. There is no such thing as time in Heaven, yet many souls stay there for up to eighty Earth years. From First Heaven souls may also look on over loved ones who remain alive on Earth. The Guardian Angels facilitate this. Whilst in First Heaven our Guardian Angel will spend some time with us reviewing our life. Eventually all souls move on to further Heavens as part of their spiritual journey".

Question: "*What are the other places in Heaven?*"
"Some souls stay in First Heaven, the place of orientation, for up to eighty Earth years although there is no such thing as time in Heaven. Other souls move quickly through First Heaven and on to further experiences in deeper Heaven. The soul is directed on a path towards their assigned place where they will be reunited with soulmates and know that they have returned to their home".

Question: "*Are soulmates people whom we were close in life?*"

Answer: "Some people we were close to are our soulmates, some are not. Those who are not will belong to other soul groups. There are many soul groups. Soulmates share that they were all born as new souls together and would be at a similar level of soul development. There is great joy when a soul returns to their spiritual home. Some soulmates will already be there. Other soulmates will still be away in human life."

Question: *"What do we do once we return to our assigned place in heaven?"*

Answer: "Soulmates share experiences from their human life on Earth. There will be further learning and reflection on the life they had. A life review with more senior beings helps souls to plan their future learning, and plan for reincarnation in another human life on Earth. Soul's work with their Guardian Angels to plan another life that will bring the opportunities and challenges they need to spiritually grow."

Question: *"What happens when we die?"*

Answer: "Your soul returns to Heaven, unless you are truly evil". Most souls return to Heaven. None of us will have led perfect lives. We all make mistakes and might have caused some harm. Heaven knows us for whom we are and loves us unconditionally".
"It matters not what religion we held, or lack of religion. We are assessed according to the progress of our soul by our deeds, good or bad". For most souls, assessment is a Life Review held at some point while we are in Heaven".

Question: *"Are we punished in the Afterlife for the hurt we caused others?"*

Answer: "All souls will have a Life Review in Heaven. For those who have led a good life, showing care for others, this will be a positive appraisal. For those who have hurt others psychologically, physically, or by lack of empathy, they will be shown how others felt who were hurt."

Question: "Is being shown the hurt we caused the end of the matter?"

Answer: "No, those souls who are good and caring will continue their spiritual progress. Those who hurt others will have to be reincarnated into another life where they can learn to cause less hurt and show empathy for others. The further life experience can be where they experience challenges. Heaven believes that souls progress more rapidly when they have a tough life. The progress of every soul development is different, and Heaven will carefully plan the soul's future learning."

Question: "Can people who have hurt others physically or psychologically avoid a difficult Life Review in Heaven?"

Answer: "Heaven expects a soul to progress by becoming more loving and caring, showing empathy for others. If souls pass across to Heaven unable to show empathy, they have much to learn to spiritually progress. Their Life Review and future spiritual lessons will be difficult. However, a religious term "Repent" refers to a person changing whilst still in life. It doesn't mean simply being sorry for the hurt they caused. It means trying to put their mind into that of the victim(s) and realising how it must have felt to be on the receiving side. It means to change their behaviour to do some good in the world for the remaining part of their physical life. Heaven should (but only God will judge) make a life review easier for souls who truly repent to become more loving and caring."

Question: "Are all souls equal in the eyes of Heaven."

Answer: "Souls who are truly evil are looked on differently. However, most souls return to Heaven at the end of physical life and souls are loved equally and of equal importance. However, souls are in many stages of development. Advanced souls will have been through many lives as human beings over thousands of years. They will have progressed by becoming more knowledgeable and becoming truly loving and caring of others, of nature, and of the environment. However, the majority of souls on planet Earth are in the early to mid-stages of spiritual development. Thet may not always show empathy, and will be more prone to hurting people, and have less regard for nature and the environment than advanced soul. Often advanced souls are just ordinary people in society. Early development souls can reach positions of political, commercial and community power because human beings need to be ruthless in gaining control over others. Yes, it is scary that many souls on Earth have much to learn, and in positions of power and control. That is why planet Earth is in an increasing state of crisis with climate change, over population, excessive fossil fuel usage, wars, and personal greed."

Question: "Do we stay the same when we reach Heaven?"

Answer: "You retain all your memories, and you retain your character. We can appear in Heaven as your physical self, or as a soul energy – appearing as a ball of light. Either way we are recognised by others for whom we are".

Question: "How do we communicate in Heaven?"
"We communicate by thought projection. This is similar to telepathy, except it is a focussed, deliberate and certain

communication. It is a more effective way to talk than spoken language. When we project a thought, a lot of information may be sent or received as a sudden knowingness by the one whom we communicate with".

Question: *"Does prayer work? Does Heaven listen to our prayers?"*
Answer: "Prayer is similar to thought projection. People must direct their prayer thoughts to God. Heaven will respond through the Angels into our feelings and intuitive knowingness, but people are not always aware of how to recognise such responses."

Question: *"How do our loved ones in Heaven look at us who are left behind in life, suffering the pain of grief?"*

Answer: "You captured the reality in your poem."

Now you're Gone
You were here yesterday,
And now you're gone, passed away,
Cruel death has victory

News came swift that you had died,
It couldn't be, I screamed, denied,
Grief took hold, I cried and cried.

There are no answers from the world around
If you'd been religious would salvation
be found?

This busy world knows not what to say,
Like an express train on their way,
Material lives, living for today.

Science claims the answers in this modern world,
Life is dust to dust, so live to the full,
Young or old, boy or girl.

My grief takes hold and overwhelming,

Bewildered, lost, darkness closing in
Can't accept won't see you again.

My eyes are blind, but you can see,
I just don't feel you near to me.
Your soul is near, you still exist,
Life's cruel illusion is a mist

Your soul is free of all the pain,
Yet you're surprised, you are the same.
Heaven is beautiful, you know that now,
Others you loved are there somehow.

Heaven is real, green valleys and trees,
Flowers caressed by gentle breeze,
Colours vivid, no pain, no fear,
A place like home made ready,
for you there.

You try to reach to tell me this,
Yet the wall between us, impenetrable mist
of material world teaching,
Souls don't exist,
Leaves me trapped in grief,
Time stops, I twist,
...and cry.

At the end of our physical life, most souls reach Heaven. We must still have some goodness in our heart, even though our life may not have been perfect. It is only the truly evil souls that are side-tracked elsewhere.

A Journey to Heaven

Feel love as energy, see colours of every flower,
Sense nature in glory, Creation's finest hour,
Love's radiant colours, as a rainbow sky,
O'er dawn and sunset, we are free to fly.

Flying onward, see colours turn pure white,

A new scene before us, beautiful and bright,
Pure radiance of the Heavenly Light.

Feel love as never known before,
Joy, elation, warm and pure,
Love, as coming home can feel
Warm embrace envelops real
Tears of joy run down our cheek,
Lost for words, no need to speak.

Simply for us, a Heaven of love,
Unconditional love that shines above,
A Oneness for all whose hearts are good,
Life's meaning revealed, and understood,
Joy in eternity, existing as love.

FIRST HEAVEN

As a Clairvoyant, I can see through to the beautiful place that some who have an near death experience briefly travel to. I call this place "First Heaven". Why? because it is the first place most of us go when we first leave our Earthly life. It is a very real, solid place, and created in the image of the Earthly home we have just left so that we can transition into the next life. There are valleys, rivers, lakes, trees, flowers, green grass. Colours are vivid and the experience of being in that place is intense and joyful. Others who have passed may be waiting to greet us, but only where there is a bond of love or warm friendship. Dogs, cats, horses, can be seen with those who cared for them in life.
We can stay in this place for a long time, although there is no real time, but only the moment of "Now".
We will then move on to further experiences, and ultimately to be reborn into another life.

I have named the first place that our soul reaches after our physical life ends: "First Heaven".

First Heaven
See light everywhere,
Gentle warmth of unconditional love
Drawn into First Heaven, somehow,
Just here, not above

Free from life on Earth
From pain, suffering, happiness, pleasure
Back to our true home, somehow familiar
Cannot measure,
.... The overwhelming love
 We can still think and see,
Loved ones who passed before,
waiting patiently
I see their faces, young again,
Together we fly free,
Across beautiful valleys, grass, trees, flowers
A very real Heaven created by the One with powers,
.................of Creation

Question: "What happens when we have a Life Review in Heaven?"

Answer: *"In the afterlife of Heaven, we will at some point have a Life Review, accompanied by our Guardian Angel. We can travel to a building that is a library."*

A Library in Heaven
Our soul set free from our body, our life,
Float on a path towards a building white,
The Heaven we hoped for shines all around
Breathe air of love, see beauty profound.

Heaven is light, love, joy and peace,
Beauty, safety, feel wonderful, at ease,
See radiant Angels, sense power,

of the Creator above
Overwhelming, infinite, unconditional love.

Heaven offers rest, to recover from life's pain,
Then time to review, start learning again.

A brilliant white building in front now see,
Is a place of further learning, a Library,
Now before you many books of life
For everyone who ever lived
their toils, their strife,
Their joy, sorrow, happiness, fun,
The times they had to fight, battles lost and won.

See a book now, with your name bold and clear,
Should you reach to grasp it?
Your Angel guide says: "Don't fear",
Each page is a day of your life we did give,
Every moment, every minute
we may view and relive.

Open a page of happiness and joy,
Go back to your childhood a girl or a boy,
Angel now guides you, in a most gentle way,
to visit a page where your life went astray.
Did you hurt others?
Were you blind but now know,
  When we hurt others, we can't spiritually grow

We can enter the page, we are in life again,
At that moment in time when we caused someone pain
We can work it through differently,
Not self-centred, but care,
Understand how others feel,
Learn how to share.

Now awake from your vision
Was this real, had you dreamed?
You're alive, not passed away,
To the afterlife that seemed ……..so real.

CHAPTER NINE

Secrets of Spiritual Communication

Question: "It seems that words can sometimes cause harm. How does Heaven view this?"

Answer: "Angels would like to remind humanity of the powerful effect of words."

Words
We use words to communicate,
We use words to learn,
Words express love and happiness,
Words also can be fun.
Words may cause harm if the truth we twist,
Barriers and opportunities missed. Words can lead to fights, suffering, and pain,
Words from self-centred people,
seeking personal gain.
Relationships take time to build,
Yet, in seconds words may destroy, despair,
Do such words ever do anything,
to get us anywhere?
Question: *How do Guardian Angels communicate with people?*

Answer: "Angels communicate through our intuitive feelings."

Intuition
Intuition emanates from our soul, our inner being,
From within the realms and depths of clear seeing.

Without eyes or words, a sense of just knowing,
The answers to problems that have been growing,
Worries in our mind, decisions to make,
Crossroads in life, the direction to take.

Intuition may come quickly, when answers hard to find,
Sudden knowingness from somewhere,
see clear, no longer blind.
Messages from Guardian Angels,
into our soul, deep within,
Mysterious whisperings, once dormant,
their guidance now begin.

Lift the veil, the link with Heaven,
Our Angels try to help,
They see a bigger picture,
the best way forward for yourself. Believe your intuition, let inner
wisdom guide,
Answers to life's problems, will come from deep inside.
Guardian Angels always with you
will help you from above,
Intuitive guidance through your life, in unconditional love.

Projecting Our Thoughts
In Heaven we speak by projecting our thought,
Perfect communication,
No need to be taught.

Language difficult, slow, a baby must learn,
In life that's how we communicate,
So important to earn,
Our place in society.

In our life as humans our thoughts we express
Through speech, and writing, no need to thought project,
Our memory of Heaven may no longer be there,
We are physical, human,

Most never think or care,
About our soul.

Our Guardian Angels from Heaven, our spiritual home,
Project thoughts to our mind, as through life we roam,
They try to guide us, on paths, life fulfilment to find,
Sense their help through our feelings
Hear their thoughts in our mind.

Projecting thoughts for our needs
Heaven will receive,
In silent prayer, to the Highest in whom we believe,
Project our thoughts in prayer to the unconditional love,
Of those trying to help us in Heaven above.

A secret of clairvoyance, pray to Heaven above,
Answers to our prayers
We will come back with their love.

CHAPTER TEN

What are paranormal phenomena?

Question to Heaven: *"Should people believe in the paranormal?"*

Answer: "Most people don't need to believe in the paranormal such as ghosts and poltergeists. Heaven protects people from paranormal phenomena. We know that some people do believe in paranormal phenomena. We will give you knowledge to explain and understand each type of phenomena."

Question: *"Do bad people stay behind to cause paranormal phenomena?"*

Answer: "When a person hurts others physically or psychologically continually in a deliberate way, their soul energy becomes darkened. What I mean by this is that our soul is a central ball of energy, surrounded by further soul energies, and it is these energies that may become dark if we committed some evil acts. If a soul still has some goodness remaining, then the person will still be allowed into Heaven, but their dark soul energies will be shed and left behind on the Earth plain. Negative energies are not allowed into Heaven. So, a soul entering Heaven with energies that have been left behind will have to restore their energies in Heaven. We all have a Life Review in Heaven. If we were a good caring person this review will be a positive experience. If we caused hurt and damage, then we will be shown this. Our spiritual progress will have been halted or even reversed and we must go through further learning and experiences to progress. Such souls will have to go back into a life, reincarnate, to experience the hurt they

caused in their previous life.
The dark energies left behind on the Earth plain by many millions of souls is the main cause of paranormal phenomena."

Question to Heaven: *"What are ghosts and poltergeists?"*

Answer: "Souls that have chosen to stay in the Earth plain, usually do so due to emotionally intense situations prior to death. These create the most active phenomena that can be witnessed and also recorded electronically. Ghosts are not necessarily evil. However, a poltergeist is a long-standing human soul ghost that has changed into something evil and with a deliberate intention to cause fright and distress."

Question to Heaven: What are paranormal energies?

Answer: "Negative Energies are paranormal. The soul has an inner core that is the "I am" and is surrounded by soul energy which can become darkened when a person causes cause harm. When a person physically dies, they cannot take dark soul energy with them. It is shed and gets left behind on the Earth plain. This dark energy has its own programmed purpose. As it did in life, it exists to cause fear and hurt on the Earth plain. It is these negative energies that can influence the souls of people in life, but only those who cause psychological or physical harm. It is by nature destructive and may cause people to stop caring about hurting others or damaging nature and the environment. Negative, dark soul energy can be highly concentrated on Earth in areas of tragedy, or areas of war. Such energy can even join to form large concentrations of negative energy that manifest as poltergeists and demons.
When a person hurts others, psychologically or physically, they are resonating at a low spiritual level. Their soul becomes open to influence by Earthbound negative energies, and they start to ignore their conscience."

Question to Heaven: "Is paranormal phenomena evidence of the soul surviving death".

Answer: "Many paranormal researchers do their work such as ghost hunting in a search for hard evidence of an afterlife and that the human soul survives physical death.

In addition, the huge increase in technology available to record paranormal phenomena has produced some astounding evidence. Camera technology, infrared and ultraviolet, smart phone cameras, EVP recordings (Electronic Voice Phenomena), spirit boxes, SLS cameras and much more show that spiritual energies can and do interact with electricity, radio waves and technology.

However, as much as paranormal phenomena manifests to create physical evidence, the souls creating this type of phenomena are in the minority. They are the souls or soul energies that remain earthbound by reason of anger, emotionally intense events or because of negative (evil) energies. Most souls (over 99%) pass safely across to a place in the afterlife that religions may describe as "Heaven". Souls in Heaven do not create paranormal phenomena but can be detected in other ways."

Phenomena that can be seen clairvoyantly, even in daylight

Souls in Heaven can spend time in a mirror image physical place or building that exists due to the Quantum particles and energies from the real building reaching into the spiritual dimension. The souls have reached First Heaven. They are not ghosts.

Mark was the leader of a paranormal group based in West Yorkshire, England who attended a café on an evening ghost hunting vigil. The café owners had purchased the business several years ago following the death of the husband-and-wife team who previously ran the café business into their old age. The new owners gave Mark accounts of a ghostly figure of a man who would appear unexpectedly to staff and customers in a full materialisation that was similar in description to the previous owner, now deceased. During the evening vigil, Mark took charge of an infra-red camera. Such cameras can capture spectrums of light that the human eye can't detect. What he caught on camera was the most convincing evidence of the evening vigil. Video taken at the area where meals were cooked and prepared clearly showed a male and a female figure busy preparing food. These were the husband-and-wife team in spirit, still doing what they always did in life, working in their much-loved café.

When I later heard about this event, I realised that the deceased still working in the café were still working in a mirror-image café created for them in the Afterlife. There are quantum energies of physical matter that act as a link passing backwards and forwards between the physical universe and the dimension of the Spiritual Realm. These quantum energies are particles that help create mirror-image buildings, and homes. This is deliberately planned by those in the Afterlife. The reason for this is that some souls who have passed cannot accept their death and need easing through a transitional soul experience that gives them familiar surroundings such as this café. If souls spend time in mirror-image buildings such as this café they can create energies that manifest in the real physical café, as was happening in this case.

Residual Phenomena

Apparitions that can be seen clairvoyantly only. These are recorded images and feelings that exist due to an emotionally intense event. The recording is held in the building, room, or area of land. It is a type of recording held in the spiritual ether in a similar way to the record of someone's life events accessed during a life review. Such phenomena could be described as residual because the souls who were involved with the emotional event have long since moved on. Manifestations of this kind are not created by current soul activity.

Ghosts & Poltergeists

Souls that have chosen to stay in the Earth plain, usually due to emotionally intense situation prior to death. These create the most active phenomena that can be witnessed and recorded electronically. Ghosts are not necessarily evil. A poltergeist is a long-standing human soul ghost that has changed into something evil and with a deliberate intention to cause fright and distress.

Poltergeist Activity

Alex was walking his dog, a German Shepard named Rex on a familiar footpath about a mile from his home in the Yorkshire Dales, England. It was a familiar walk for Alex. Over the other side of a dry-stone wall, so common in the Dales, he could see the old stone quarry, long since abandoned. There were many scary accounts of sightings of strange spiritual phenomena at the old quarry, but Alex had never experienced anything. He was a sceptic concerning ghosts. The time of year was late November. Winter had set in and there was a cold bite to the air. The time was five pm and darkness had arrived as he decided to turn around and head back home. Suddenly his dog Rex started to become agitated and began to bark with his attention directed towards the nearby quarry. What Alex saw next would stay with him for the rest of his life. A large white energy appeared and rose-up from inside the quarry. The energy appeared with head and a body but was most certainly not human. The size of the spiritual manifestation was huge, much bigger than a two-storey house. It continued to rise-up from the quarry and seemed to see him, moving towards him and Rex. Alex ran. He dared not look behind as he ran home with Rex at his side. Since then, Alex has walked his dog many times up near the old quarry. Rex always becomes agitated when they near the quarry, but Alex has not seen the manifestation since. Perhaps because he would never walk there in the dark again.

This is an example of poltergeist activity. This type of manifestation usually occurs on a site where there has been human death and suffering. Negative spiritual energies, generated by human suffering, can stay, lingering, especially where the land has been damaged such as in the area of a quarry. Negative spiritual energies have a consciousness that is not human that seems to manifest deliberately to cause distress and fear to unsuspecting passers-by. You will read later in this book more detail concerning the nature of negative spiritual energies.

Don was walking down a side street in London one evening. He noticed a small crowd of people stood around a shoe shop window. The shop was closed for business, but the shop display window was well lit. To Don's amazement he could see what was drawing the attention of the other people in the crowd. Shoes in the display window were being picked-up as of by some unseen hand and were drifting through the air to land at the other side of the display. The manifestation continued for around fifteen minutes then suddenly stopped. No-one watching could explain what had happened, and the crowd gradually dispersed. This is a further example of poltergeist activity. The manifestation is caused by negative energies that are linked to the physical site of the shop. No doubt the energies would have been generated by human death and suffering that happened on the site of the shoe shop, perhaps many years earlier.

There are several types of haunting and not all are the same. Fortunately, I encountered some of the different kinds of haunting all in one location, as described in the following true account:

In February 2013, I visited one of the most haunted houses in York, on Stonegate, a well-known street in the main tourist shopping area. I was just a paying participant of an overnight vigil organised by one of the well-known companies who organise ghost hunting events. I arrived at 8pm for a 9pm start and was told to wait outside. Later, as the time approached 9pm I was surprised at how many people had booked to attend this evening. Entering this house with small rooms was a party more than 30 people, each paying over £50, so my first impression was of commercial greed compromising the ideal situation of a smaller number of participants in a ghost hunting vigil.

However, the residual and active spiritual energies in this house proved fascinating. The first discovery I made was that several of the different types of hauntings were very strongly manifest and provide excellent examples.

I kept quiet for an hour or so that I am clairvoyant... although it did come out before the night was over in quite a dramatic way.

The guest clairvoyant was speaking about a monk, who haunted the house, because the site had once been a monastery. I could clairvoyantly see the monk who seemed quite harmless, stood in a corner. He remained harmless through the evening. However, as we were grouping together on the first floor, I clairvoyantly saw a wild-eyed man with unkempt black hair come charging through the door. He looked crazed. I asked my angel guide who he was. I was told that he had spent several years fighting overseas, around the late 18th century, and had returned home completely mad and quite violent. Back to the real world, and the ghost hunt leader was explaining that in this room objects were often thrown around. I knew who was throwing them, but I said nothing.

So, this is an example of a grounded spirit, still earthbound because the circumstances of his life had turned him into a madman. Why don't the angels rescue such souls? I don't have all the answers.

The group were next led downstairs into the cellar/ basement. As a group of around 30 people, we were all forced into a very tiny room area. I got myself positioned into a corner of the room. "This is at the level of the street in Roman times and is where Roman Legion soldiers in ghostly form have been seen marching." I clairvoyantly looked around for Roman soldiers, but there were none. Such apparitions usually concur with a date or a time of year when some emotionally charged event happened, in this case way back 2000 years ago. However, I did hear a voice whispering to me in some old language. It was a male voice, repeating the same words repeatedly. Was it Nordic? ... the Vikings had captured and ruled over York. Was the language Roman, or even old English? I said to my angel guide in my thoughts "Please translate". The voice immediately became clear with the words "Help me", Help me", repeated. Was this some poor soul grounded for more than 1000 years? I didn't get chance to find out as we were ushered back upstairs to a small room overlooking Stonegate.

They switched the lights out in this small room. We all stood quietly. "Can anyone tell me if they feel or sense anything" the ghost hunt leader asked. No-one said anything. Well, "Here goes...", I thought to myself, clearly seeing a cot in the room from sometime around 150 years ago. "A baby died in her cot in this room," I said. The leader replied "Oh, that could be right, this room is known for the ghostly sound of a baby crying."

The baby crying is an example of residual energy. I had also seen and sensed a family around her, who were poor, and cold during winter.

We were then led upstairs to a large, panelled room with a huge round table that could seat approximately 20 people. Many of our party sat down, but I was one of the ten who had to stand. The event leader, a woman aged perhaps late fifties, came up to me and whispered, "What do you sense?" I told her that I could see clairvoyantly that this was a male meeting room. Women were not allowed in here, and women may still feel uncomfortable because there is a male watch-keeper in spirit telling any woman to get out. "That's right," our leader said. "This room was used for Masonic meetings." During our vigil in the room the guest clairvoyant tried to summon the spirits to do table tipping, but the table didn't move. The ghost hunting team picked up a voice on the EVP monitor saying, "Get out!", and the EMF meters kept flashing. Clairvoyantly I could see two simultaneous meetings of men being re-enacted. Both ghostly meetings were ignoring each other and ignoring us. The earliest dated meeting I could see was of men wearing wigs, possibly early 19th century, but I'm no historian. The meeting was emotionally charged because this group of men were mourning the loss of colleagues in some war, possibly fighting the French. There were empty seats, and the meeting was very sad and reflective, but being re-lived in spirit. The second meeting was of men sat in the same places, but from a later period, possibly late 19th century. They were all dressed in black suits and following very serious ritualistic procedures. Just why their meeting was still being re-enacted I couldn't get an answer to, but the emotions were dark, strict and of disciplinary fear.

We were then given a break. I went to the gents' toilet and spoke briefly to another attendee who said he had been on a few of these ghost hunts. "It must be exciting," I said. "Not really," he replied. "I haven't ever seen anything ghostly, and it gets a bit boring." After the break we found ourselves being led further up narrow, uneven stairs to then be split up into smaller groups, each spending time in smaller rooms higher up. I was led with about eight others into a room where I immediately saw a very angry man, still grounded there in spirit. I asked him in my mind why he was angry. He told me that himself, his wife and children had all caught the plague and were forced to stay in the room. It was very hot, with no ventilation, and they had little food or water. The children had died first, then his wife, and then he had died. We were going back in time to the 17th or 18th century. I said nothing while the ghost hunt leader set up a table to try to get "The spirits" to do table tipping. I volunteered to put my fingers gently on the table, as did a few others. "If there are any spirits here then show us your presence!" exclaimed the leader. Nothing happened despite several repeated exclamations. I thought to myself that I had to say something. "Look, there is a man in spirit over in the corner who is very angry. Can I ask him to tip the table?" "Yes"... in an uncertain voice said the leader. So, I said, "Look, I can see you are angry, please move the table." The table started to immediately rotate strongly in a clockwise direction. The floor surface was uneven, but the table rotated firmly as though nothing could stop it. It didn't in any way seem frightening. "Ok, show us how really angry you are by making this table tip!" With that request the table lifted into the air and crashed sideways onto the floor. Others from nearby rooms came rushing-in due to the loud bang as the table hit the deck, and the lights were put back on.

We then were ushered upstairs into the attic. I was now suddenly surrounded by team members holding equipment near me as I gave an account of a cleaning lady who used to clean up this area, which had at one time been used as a grain store. However, in my vision I was then taken right back in time, prior to the house being built, prior to the monastery that had been on that site. There were big stones raining down on me, crushing those who had been on this site. Giant catapults were being used as huge weapons of battle to sling stones at those below in some battle. Was this from Viking times, or from Roman times? Again, I am no historian. This was simply residual energy capturing a very emotionally charged moment in history when many were injured and died.

I left the overnight vigil early, at 3pm. The final activity for the attendees was to conduct a seance, and I don't participate in seances. My reason is that during a seance we are inviting any spirit to make contact or do something. It can open the door, bring down our defences to dark spirits, and I don't do that.

Photographic evidence of ghosts

Photography can pick up a wider spectrum of light than the human eye. At one end of the light spectrum, we have ultra-violet light (UV). However, most cameras are fitted with a UV filter. This simply filters out UV light.

At the other end of the spectrum there is infra-red light. Some cameras are specially adapted to recorded infra-red light. The infra-red spectrum is recorded as heat signature.

Ghosts can often be recorded on camera when they were otherwise invisible to the naked eye.

Negative (evil) energies

These are soul energies shed by human souls who allowed their soul energy to become dark.

Such energies have a consciousness and can meld with other negative soul energies to become a larger energy and manifest as demons or poltergeists that are attached to physical places, especially buildings, and often over an area of land such as the site of a battle in war where many lives were lost.

Question to Heaven: "Can a soul stay Earthbound having been through emotional distress?"

Answer: "Please find your answer in the following poem"

CHRISTMAS EVE
Christmas Eve, dark, and cold outside,
Our family gather at this yule tide.
Our manor house is warm and bright,
Good food and wine, candles, fire light.

A knock resounded on front door,
Our servant answered "I implore,
there's a young girl Sir, who begs your time"
"I will speak with her when I've finished my wine"
The girl looked pale, her clothes but rags,
her shoes were worn, two empty bags.

"Please Sir, have you food to spare?
my mother is ill, my father not there,
He died last year, I have sisters three,
We are but children, will you help me?"
"We live in the cottage, near the old well,
There is no road, no-one to tell"

I said: "Fill her bags with bread and meat,
vegetables, cakes, so they can eat"
"May your mother get well, see her I will,

In New Year to help through winter chill"

"What is your name?" I gently asked.
"My name is Alison Grey, I do all the tasks,
I am the eldest child, you see,
My brother died, now it's up to me"

Young Alison left, and gave her thanks,
Into dark night, snow on high banks.
Come New Years Day, we went for a walk,
Cold winter sun, my wife and I talked,
Of the poor family of Alison Grey,
"We must pay them a visit, It's over this way"

I remember the cottage, near the old well,
I'd not been there in years, my wife did me tell.
Footpath overgrown, "Oh, those poor souls unknown,
How had they lived there, on their own?"

We passed through the wood, it was darker, tall trees,
The sunshine was hidden, I felt the cold breeze,
Then, out to a clearing, we'd reached the old well,
The cottage was empty, no-one there I could tell.

It was then that we saw graves almost hidden away,
A headstone: "Here lies the body of Alison Grey",
She had died ten years earlier, on Christmas Day.

CHAPTER ELEVEN

Animals and Nature

Angels work constantly in Nature. The tell us that an important spiritual quality is to be loving and caring towards others, towards, animals, and nature and the environment. It is a measure of our spiritual growth.

Daffodil
Oh daffodil, your beauty of moment,
Last forever if time never spent.

All year you hide away from sight,
To appear in gardens as Springtime Light

Yellow radiance as the sun,
In coat of green your leaves are spun

Soft breeze caress, you move and dance,
Flower of love, colour of romance

You are Spring, and Spring is you,
You are my image of life renew.

My spirit lifts with you nearby,
I scarce can turn away my eye.

Oh daffodil, your beauty of moment,
And eternal dreams forever dreamt.

Animals and Birds have a soul energy, not as big as a human soul, but still loved by God.

Little Bird

Little bird, on a tree branch up there,
Singing your song across the air,
A message to other birds, I am sure,
To me your song is pleasant and pure.
Little bird always seeking food to eat,
Then flying away to your safe retreat,
Little bird, you know how to make your nest,
Raise your young, and look your best,
Little bird, little bird, on a tree branch, up there,
Singing your song across the air
You know love, you have a soul,
I know you're aware...

Question: "Do Angels work to support nature?"

Answer: "Captured in the following poem"

Grasmere Cumbria

Serene, beautiful, calm, majestic
Inspirational, classical, peaceful, poetic
All these feelings as I walked your path side,
A mere not a lake, your calm water's wide
Deer Bolts Wood I roam, evening creeps up on me,
Darkness comes quickly, I cared not, I was free,
Of city life, suburban jungle, not really me.

Warm caress of summer evening, sky melted to a glow,
Of fiery red between high mountains, natures beauty show
I wander now towards the village, warm hotel to be my host,
Then I saw a light before me, my mind perplexed, was this a ghost?
A light of white and strange in darkness, moving yet there was no breeze,
Floating above, across the mere, meandering back into the trees,
Was this the soul of classical poet whose heart belonged to this fine place?

Still dwells amongst this place of magic, where early Springtime daffodils grace?

I felt no fear as light approached me, I was a stranger in fairy land.
I had to know, I had to ask, who are you? my need to understand,
Then a whispering voice around me, from the water and the land
"I am no ghost of classical poet, he was my friend, he knew me well,
I am an Angel, to care for nature, the woods, the animals, 'tis here I dwell".

"This is a place of Angels, love, and healing through eternity,
This evening, now, a special moment, all of life in harmony,
Remember this for all your years, know how precious life can be,
Please try to work to save our planet, for poets of old, for you and me."

Question to Heaven: "Do Animals have a soul?"

Answer: *"Yes, animals have a soul. All animals that show emotions have a soul energy."*

Life of a Dog
Brought him home as a puppy, all timid and meek,
But it wasn't too long before havoc did wreak,
He would tear around, with energy abound,
Light up with joy as he played with a toy,
When bored with that he'd play chasing the cat
He got into trouble, turned tail on the double,
When I found he'd dare chew the back of my chair.
Now that he is older, house-trained he be,
He sits when he's told, on leash stays near me,
When walking, if I shout, he'll stop, and he'll see,
To come running without doubt, from wherever he be.
He acts as a guard dog, alert day and night,
I'm sure of confronted he'll defend family alright.

As I go out to work, he looks sad and bored,
When I come home, he seems overjoyed,
The welcome he gives, and the fuss that he makes,
Can be a little too much if I'm tired and ache.
When I think of my dog, I can say without doubt,
There's a personality in there,
Not just animal looking out.
When I look in his eyes, he cannot disguise,
The affection and trust, and loyalty,
The truest of animal friends to me.

Question: Do Animals go to Heaven?

Answer: "The soul of an animal returns to a different Heaven to that of a human being. Where a person and animal were close in life, the animal soul can go to the human Heaven to be with the person in Heaven who cared for them".

A Soul Within Animals
Little bird, enchanting song, perching on your tree,
Your tiny eyes look out, yes, you notice me.
My pet dog is so lovable, I see happiness in his play,
He shows anger at a stranger, sadness when I'm away.
How can my dog show emotions?
Animal is his nature,
Might the world believe all life has soul,
sometime in the future?
Religions might say animals have no soul,
Science says their brain inside,
is nothing more than flesh, spiritual nature denied.

I often feel that I can fly, or feel powerful like a lion,
I feel a part of nature, yet I am a human being,
I am clairvoyant and questions ask, not to this world so wide,
I ask questions to the Angels,
Answers come back from the other side ..of life.
Do birds and animals have a soul?

All life in nature too?
What is the human soul?
The response was surprising and new.
Our spirit comes in small drops,
like an ocean wide,
All living creatures have small drops, of soul energy inside.
After many lives experience, in life of every form,
Small drops of spirit converge, one larger soul reborn.
Souls of a thousand living things, come together just as one,
Emerging as a human soul, a new oneness now begun.
The human soul is bigger than animal, that cannot be denied,
Yet, when my dog looks in my eyes,
I know he has a soul inside.

CHAPTER TWELVE

Planet Earth

The following poems about *Planet Earth* have been inspired by conversations with Heaven.

Life, where are you going?
Life, where are you going? as river, onward flowing,
Twisting left, meandering right, different ways, new paths in sight
New things to do, feelings renew.

When the river flows calm and wide,
All seems well on life's journey ride,
River moves faster, playful dance,
Tumbling over rocks, scattered by chance,
Life moves faster, heart beats faster too,
We're high then low, happy, then blue.

Then, dance is echoed by thunder sound,
Inside apprehension, roar all around,
River tumbles down rapid falls,
No more, calm, rage crashing calls.
Life's storms will also come our way,
No matter sun or rainy day,
We're torn in half, emotional pain,
No calm, no harmony again?

Then, still and clear, fresh waters reach
In life new light, new hope, beseech.

Life, where are you going, full circle again?
Or some new twist in your hidden game?
As river meanders to distant sea,
Life's good times, and bad, steer my destiny,
With my love for nature, and our planet Earth
Guiding me.

Question: "What is it that calls souls to have a Life on Earth?"

Answer: *"The Beauty of our precious planet"*

Walking
A gentle Spring morning, the sun and blue sky,
delicate white clouds, floating high,
Walk up a steep path, into the trees,
Tall branches filtered sun, calm shelter from breeze.

A timeless rustling of leaves, restless movements of air,
As the wind high above rushed to who knows where,
Wildflowers of blue, lilac, yellow around,
Birds singing above, their own sweet sound.

Feel at peace with the world, aware of creation,
A beautiful, warm, uplifting sensation.

Wander endlessly on, not once will we tire,
'Till end of day comes, the sky alive with fire,
The red, orange and purple, its beauty show,
Sunset o'er distant mountains, melt into a glow.

Pray for our world, and felt heightened awareness,
 soul in harmony with creation,
Through nature's sweet caress.

Question: "Is there such a thing as a Portal to Heaven?"

Answer: "Captured in the following poem."

Derwent Water, Cumbria

Enchanted places on Earth
have many portals to Heaven,
Derwentwater, Cumbria is a place of them.

I walked an easy path, through trees on Friar's Cragg
My spirit now uplifted, my weary feet didn't drag,
Then, before my eyes unfolded the lake, and Borrowdale,
Morning mist and distant mountains
rose-up to tell a tale,
Of majesty and wonder that many authors inspire
Poetic feelings intense, awakened, hearts that burnt on fire,
To rest in this place forever, so many would desire.

I spoke with my Guardian Angel, felt harmony inside,
With all of life in nature. Joy I could not hide.

A portal travels both ways, for those in Heaven
can still see,
This precious view that they experienced,
when they were alive and free.

I see them with my clairvoyant gift,
I hear the words that they once wrote,
This place enchanted, I see more Angels,
The moment forever caught,
In my soul, my very being,
That will live through eternity,
I will return someday in spirit,
Heaven on Earth is where I'll be.

CLIMATE CHANGE

Burn, burn, burn, oil, gas, coal and wood,
Burn, burn, burn,
Forests, and places where houses stood.

Drown, drown, drown, storms that rarely came before,
Air temperatures rise, precipitation more,
Drown, drown, drown, crops submerged, fields now lakes,
Houses flooded for our mistakes.

World industrial machine, once a dream,
Powers relentlessly on, answers to none.

Our emissions will be zero, greenhouse gasses are a cause,
Some countries won't comply, nation leaders meet, verbal wars.

Somewhere in our world, fossil fuels burn, no control,
The actions of a few, will impact on us all.

Burn, burn, until fossil fuel reserves end,
Politicians may talk and recommend,
Without real action, climate change won't mend.
Can nations stop temperature rise?
Just watching,
While a large part of nature dies.

I Fell Asleep
I fell asleep,
When I awoke it was Covid,
Not allowed in street
So, I fell asleep.

I awoke, and the third antichrist.
Russia in Ukraine, atrocities, sliced,
Not my problem
So, I fell asleep.

I awoke to storms, floods, climate change,

My house was dry, floods out of range,
So, I fell asleep.

I awoke, not climate again! famine and drought,
I was tired and couldn't be bothered,
Best keep out,
So, I fell asleep.

I awoke to nuclear wars,
Conflict of superpowers
What could I do?
So, I fell asleep,
For the last time.

Death of Nature

From trees and plants that lived and died, through millions of years,
My treasure hidden underground, away from human wars and tears,
I am fossil fuels, long dormant,
I have been waiting for this time,
Of resurrection by humanity
On their evolution climb.

Stored from death of nature long ago,
Forests died, forming coal, oil below.

Captured sun that shone on Jurassic lands,
Now making fire at people's command
To power industry, cars, boats, and planes
Human beings unaware of my end game
From death of forests and life, during eras long ago,
Destruction to nature, my flames now released, in one go.

My fire, my energy abused,
Coal, oil, and gas, overused,
I bring climate change, pollution,
Death to nature, pain, confusion.

Plastics in oceans,
Polluted cities, toxic air,
Can nature recover?
Fossil fuels don't care.

CHAPTER THIRTEEN

Seeing the Future

Question: "The Angels tell me that Heaven knows some of our future. What is the secret?"

 Answer: "The following Insight from the Angels is just one of many ways that Heaven sees our future."

Seeing The Future
What If...
The big things in our future are determined in our past,
Free Will just takes care of our everyday tasks.

We have no memory of past lives that made us whom we are,
Yet, deep-down feelings inside somehow seem to draw...
Our lives in a certain direction every time
Life can be good, can be hard, not always fine.

Our Guardian Angels know our Life Plan,
Whom we'll be, whom we'll meet,
The places we will live, every town, every street.

If we live a bad life, our Guardian Angels won't be near,
We feel uncertain of the future, lives over-shadowed by fear,
If we stray from our Life Plan, make mistakes, go astray,
This is shown to us in Life Review, at the end of Life's Day

Try to be closer to our Guardian Angels,
We can do this by gaining empathy,
for people, for nature... feel love and humility,

Our Guardian Angel now with us, unconditional love will set us free.

Intuitive visions of our future,
Two paths ahead will come to see,
We can change a path of pain,
to a path of joy...true destiny

Mind thoughts are racing, if only we truly knew
This poem still holds a secret,
"What Ifs" can really be true.

Question: "What will the world be like in the year 2100?"

Answer: "We can see the future. The story of the twenty-first century is already unfolding as we experience the real effects of climate change on our weather systems. Storms are becoming stronger, and floods, drought and wildfires are more frequent and severe."

The Year 2100
I look back on the twenty-first century,
As no other ingrained in the memory
Of humankind
No longer eight billion souls alive
Just four billion people survive.
Can I but tell you how so many died?
Climate change brought storms, crop failure, starvation,
Fossil fuels gone, famine in every nation,
Mass food production fertiliser, chemicals transport
Laid bare the soil, poisoned nature, environment hurt.

No fuel for our machines that made, we must work by hand,
Our material goods in short supply, people can't understand,
This is a new future.

Please see my website supporting "Conversations with Heaven": www.angelsxyz.com

Printed in Great Britain
by Amazon

29970908R00046